Effortle[illegible] Air Fryer Poultry Recipes

A Collection of Tasty and Affordable Poultry Recipes for Air Fryer

By Donna Thomson

The content within this book has been derived from various sources. Please consult a licensed professional before attempting any techniques outlined in this book.

By reading this document, the reader agrees that under no circumstances is the author responsible for any losses, direct or indirect, which are incurred as a result of the use of information contained within this document, including, but not limited to, — errors, omissions, or inaccuracies.

Table of Contents

Garlic Paprika Rubbed Chicken Breasts

Serves: 4

Cooking Time: 30 Minutes

Ingredients:

- 1 tablespoon stevia powder /15G
- 2 tablespoons fresh lemon juice, freshly squeezed /30ML
- 2 tablespoons Spanish paprika /30G
- 2 teaspoons minced garlic /10G
- 3 tablespoons extra virgin olive oil /45ML
- 4 boneless chicken breasts
- Salt and pepper to taste

Instructions:

1) Preheat the air fryer for 5 minutes.
2) Place all ingredients inside a baking dish. Stir to mix.
3) Place the chicken pieces in the air fryer.
4) Cook for 30 minutes at 325° F or 163°C .

Nutrition information:

- Calories per serving:424
- Carbohydrates: 3.9g
- Protein: 62.2g
- Fat: 17.7g

Garlic Rosemary Roasted Chicken

Serves: 6

Cooking Time: 50 minutes

Ingredients:

- 1 tsp rosemary /5G
- 2 pounds whole chicken /900G
- 4 cloves of garlic, minced
- Salt and pepper to taste

Instructions:

1) Season the whole chicken well with garlic, salt, and pepper.
2) Place inside air fryer basket.
3) Cook for 30 Minutes at 330° F or 166°C .
4) Flip the chicken and cook for another 20 minutes.

Nutrition information:

- Calories per serving: 328
- Carbohydrates: 30.8g
- Protein: 14.5g
- Fat: 16.3g

Ginger Garam Masala Rubbed Chicken

Serves: 4

Cooking Time: 50 minutes

Ingredients:

- 1 bell pepper, seeded and julienned
- 1 cup coconut milk /250ML
- 1 teaspoon coriander powder /5G
- 1 teaspoon garam masala /5G
- 1 teaspoon turmeric powder /5G
- 1 thumb-size ginger, grated
- 1 whole chicken, sliced into
- 2 tablespoons essential olive oil /30ML

Instructions:

1) Preheat mid-air fryer for 5 minutes.
2) Place all ingredients in the baking dish.
3) Stir to combine completely.
4) Place inside the air fryer.
5) Cook for 50 minutes at 350° F or 177°C .

Nutrition information:

- Calories per serving: 699
- Carbohydrates: 4.9g
- Protein: 44.5g

- Fat: 55.7g

Greens 'n Turkey sausage Frittata

Servings per Recipe: 2

Cooking Time: 20 Minutes

Ingredients:

- ½ cup cheddar cheese finely grated, extra sharp /65G
- ½ cup milk skimmed /125ML
- 1/2-pound breakfast turkey sausage /225G
- 1/4 tsp cayenne /1.25G
- 1/4 tsp garlic powder /1.25G
- 2-oz hash browns frozen, shredded /60G
- 3 eggs
- 5-oz pre-cut mixed greens (kale, spinach, swiss chard or other things that are you will find) /150G
- green onions for serving
- salt to taste

Instructions:

1) Lightly oil the baking pan of the air fryer with cooking spray and add turkey sausage.
2) For 5 minutes, cook on 360° F or 183°C . Cut the sausage in half.
3) Whisk eggs in a bowl. Season with salt, cayenne, and garlic powder. Add milk and whisk well.

4) Remove the basket and cut more sausage. Stir in frozen hash brown and continue cooking for 5 minutes.
5) Toss in mixed greens and cheese.
6) Pour egg mixture over hash brown mixture.
7) Cook for an additional 10 minutes until eggs are cooked.
8) Sprinkle green onions and let it sit for a minute.
9) Serve and enjoy.

Nutrition Information:

- Calories per Serving: 616
- Carbs: 39.8g
- Protein: 39.7g
- Fat: 33.1g

Grilled Chicken Pesto

Servings per Recipe: 8

Cooking Time: 30 Minutes

Ingredients:

- 1 ¾ cup commercial pesto /208G
- 8 chicken thighs
- Salt and pepper to taste

Instructions:

1) Place all Ingredients within the Ziploc bag and allow to marinate in the fridge for some hours.
2) Preheat mid-air fryer to 390° F or 199°C .
3) Place the grill pan accessory inside the air fryer.
4) Grill the chicken for about half an hour.
5) Flip the chicken every 10 minutes for even grilling.

Nutrition information:

- Calories per serving: 477
- Carbs: 3.8g
- Protein: 32.6g
- Fat: 36.8g

Grilled Chicken Recipe From Jamaica

Servings per Recipe: 2

Cooking Time: 30 Minutes

Ingredients:

- ¼ cup pineapple chunks /32.5G
- 1 tablespoon vegetable oil /15ML
- 2 whole chicken thighs
- 3 teaspoons lime juice /15ML
- 4 tablespoons jerk seasoning /60G

Instructions:

1) Mix well all ingredients in a bowl. Marinate inside the refrigerator for 3 hours.
2) Thread chicken pieces and pineapples alternatively in skewers. Place on skewer rack in the air fryer.
3) For half an hour, cook at 360° F or 183°C . turn skewer after half the cooking time has passed.
4) Serve and enjoy.

Nutrition Information:

- Calories per Serving: 579
- Carbs: 36.3g
- Protein: 25.7g
- Fat: 36.7g

Grilled Chicken Recipe from Korea

Servings per Recipe: 4

Cooking Time: 30 Minutes

Ingredients:

- ½ cup gochujang /65G
- ½ teaspoon fresh ground black pepper /2.5G
- 1 scallion, sliced thinly
- 1 teaspoon salt /5G
- 2 pounds chicken wings /900G

Instructions:

1) Put the chicken wings in a Ziploc bag, add salt, pepper, and gochujang sauce. Mix to combine all ingredients.
2) Allow to marinate within the fridge for at least a couple of hours.
3) Preheat mid-air fryer to 390° F or 199°C .
4) Place the grill pan accessory inside the air fryer.
5) Grill the chicken wings for 30 minutes making certain to turn over the chicken after every 10 minutes of grilling.
6) Add scallions to the top and serve with additional gochujang.

Nutrition information:

- Calories per serving: 278

- Carbs: 0.8g
- Protein: 50.1g
- Fat: 8.2g

Grilled Chicken Recipe from Morocco

Servings per Recipe: 4

Cooking Time: 20 Minutes

Ingredients:

- 1-pound skinless, boneless chicken thighs, cut into 2" pieces /450G
- 2 garlic cloves, chopped
- 2 teaspoons ground cumin /10G
- 2 teaspoons paprika /10G
- 3 tablespoons plain yogurt /45ML
- 4 garlic cloves, finely chopped
- Kosher salt
- Kosher salt
- Vegetable oil (for grilling)
- Warm pita bread, labneh (Lebanese strained yogurt), chopped tomatoes, and fresh mint leaves (for serving)
- 1/2 cup finely chopped fresh flat-leaf parsley /65G
- 1/3 cup organic olive oil /83ML
- 1/4 teaspoon crushed red pepper flakes /32.5G

Instructions:

1) Blend the garlic, salt, and oil until creamy. Add yogurt and continue blending until emulsified. Transfer to a bowl set aside inside a fridge.

2) Soak chicken in red pepper flakes, paprika, cumin, parsley, and garlic. Marinate for several hours in the refrigerator.
3) Thread chicken in skewers and set in the skewer rack of the air fryer.
4) Cook at 390° F or 199°C for 10 minutes. Turnover skewers after 5 minutes of cooking.
5) Use dip for side, serve and enjoy.

Nutrition Information:

- Calories per Serving: 343
- Carbs: 8.1g
- Protein: 28.0g
- Fat: 22.0g

Grilled Chicken Wings with Curry-Yogurt Sauce

Servings per Recipe: 4

Cooking Time: 35 minutes

Ingredients:

- ½ cup plain yogurt /125ML
- 1 tablespoon curry powder /15G
- 2 pounds chicken wings /900G
- Salt and pepper to taste

Instructions:

1) Season the chicken wings with yogurt, curry powder, salt and pepper. Mix properly to combine everything.
2) Allow to marinate in the fridge for about 120 minutes.
3) Preheat the air fryer to 390° F or 199°C .
4) Place the grill pan accessory in the air fryer.
5) Grill the chicken for 35 minutes and flip the chicken halfway through cooking time.

Nutrition information:

- Calories per serving: 301
- Carbs: 3.3g
- Protein: 51.3g
- Fat: 9.2g

Grilled Thighs with Honey Balsamic Sauce

Servings per Recipe: 8

Cooking Time: 40 minutes

Ingredients:

- 1/3 cup honey /83ML
- 2 tablespoons balsamic vinegar /30ML
- 2 tablespoons butter /30G
- 3 cloves of garlic, minced
- 8 bone-in chicken thighs
- Chopped chives for garnish
- Lemon wedges for garnish
- Salt and pepper to taste

Instructions:

1) Season the chicken with salt and pepper to taste. Add the butter, balsamic vinegar, honey, and garlic. Allow to marinate for 120 minutes inside the fridge.
2) Preheat mid-air fryer to 390° F or 199°C .
3) Place the grill pan accessory in the air fryer.
4) Put the chicken on the grill pan and cook for 40 minutes. Flip the chicken every 10 minutes to grill evenly.
5) Meanwhile, squeeze the remaining marinade in a saucepan and allow it to simmer until thickened.

6) Once cooked, brush the chicken with the sauce and garnish it with chives and lemon wedges.

Nutrition information:

- Calories per serving: 524
- Carbs: 32.4g
- Protein: 25.1g
- Fat: 32.7g

Healthy Turkey Shepherd's Pie

Servings per Recipe: 2

Cooking Time: 50 minutes

Ingredients:

- 1 tablespoon butter, room temperature /15G
- 1/2 clove garlic, minced
- 1/2 large carrot, shredded
- 1/2 onion, chopped
- 1/2 teaspoon chicken bouillon powder /2.5G
- 1/2-pound ground turkey /225G
- 1/8 teaspoon dried thyme /0.625G
- 1-1/2 large potatoes, peeled
- 1-1/2 teaspoons all-purpose flour /7.5G
- 1-1/2 teaspoons chopped fresh parsley /7.5G
- 1-1/2 teaspoons organic olive oil /7.5ML
- 2 tablespoons warm milk /30ML
- 4.5-ounce can sliced mushrooms /135G
- ground black pepper to taste
- salt to taste

Instructions:

1) Boil potatoes. Drain and transfer to a bowl. Mash with milk and butter until creamy. Set aside.

2) Grease a baking pan of air fryer with organic olive oil. Add onion and cook for 5 minutes, at 360° F or 183°C . Add chicken bouillon, garlic, thyme, parsley, mushrooms, carrot, and ground turkey. Cook for additional 10 minutes while stirring and mashing halfway through cooking time.
3) Season with pepper and salt. Stir in flour and mix well. Cook for two minutes.
4) Evenly spread turkey mixture. Top with mashed potatoes.
5) Cook for 20 minutes or until potatoes are lightly browned.
6) Serve and enjoy.

Nutrition Information:

- Calories per Serving: 342
- Carbs: 38.0g
- Protein: 18.3g
- Fat: 12.9g

Honey & Sriracha Over Chicken

Servings per Recipe: 4

Cooking Time: 40 minutes

Ingredients:

- ½ teaspoon garlic powder /2.5G
- ½ teaspoon paprika /2.5G
- 1 tablespoon honey /15ML
- 1 teaspoon Dijon mustard /5G
- 2 tablespoons sriracha /30ML
- 3 tablespoons rice vinegar /45ML
- 4 chicken breasts
- Salt and pepper to taste

Instructions:

1) Put all ingredients in a Ziploc bag, close the zip, mix the ingredients inside the Ziploc bag. Place in a fridge for 2 hours to allow it to marinate.
2) Preheat the air fryer to 390° F or 199°C .
3) Place the grill pan accessory within the air fryer.
4) Grill the chicken for 40 minutes or more and flip the chicken every 10 minutes for even cooking.

Nutrition information:

- Calories per serving: 510

- Carbs: 6.1g
- Protein: 60.8g
- Fat: 26.9g

Honey, Lime, And Garlic Chicken BBQ

Servings per Recipe: 4

Cooking Time: 40 minutes

Ingredients

- ¼ cup lime juice, freshly squeezed /62.5ML
- ½ cup cilantro, chopped finely /32.5G
- ½ cup honey /125ML
- 1 tablespoon organic olive oil /15ML
- 2 cloves of garlic, minced
- 2 pounds boneless chicken breasts /900G
- 2 tablespoons soy sauce /30ML
- Salt and pepper to taste

Instructions:

1) Place all ingredients in the Ziploc bag and mix all ingredients to combine well. Place in a fridge for some hours.
2) Preheat the air fryer to 390° F or 199°C .
3) Place the grill pan in the air fryer.
4) Grill the chicken for 40 minutes and turn over the chicken every 10 minutes to grill evenly on every side.

Nutrition information:

- Calories per serving: 458

- Carbs: 38.9g
- Protein:52.5 g
- Fat: 10.2g

Honey-Balsamic Orange Chicken

Servings per Recipe: 3

Cooking Time: 40 minutes

Ingredients:

- ½ cup balsamic vinegar /125ML
- ½ cup honey /125ML
- 1 ½ pounds boneless chicken breasts, pounded /675G
- 1 tablespoon orange zest /15G
- 1 teaspoon fresh oregano, chopped /5G
- 2 tablespoons extra virgin olive oil /30ML
- Salt and pepper to taste

Instructions:

1) First put the chicken inside a Ziploc bag and add the other ingredients, shake well to combine. Place in the refrigerator for two hours.
2) Preheat the air fryer to 390° F or 199°C .
3) Place the grill pan in the air fryer.
4) Grill the chicken for 40 minutes.

Nutrition information:

- Calories per serving: 521
- Carbs: 56.1g
- Protein: 51.8g

- Fat: 9.9g

Lebanese Style Grilled Chicken

Servings per Recipe: 3

Cooking Time: 20 Minutes

Ingredients:

- 1 onion, cut into large chunks
- 1 small green bell pepper, cut into large chunks
- 1 teaspoon tomato paste /5ML
- 1/2 cup chopped fresh flat-leaf parsley /65G
- 1/2 teaspoon dried oregano /2.5G
- 1/3 cup plain yogurt /83ML
- 1/8 teaspoon ground allspice /0.625G
- 1/8 teaspoon ground black pepper /0.625G
- 1/8 teaspoon ground cardamom /0.625G
- 1/8 teaspoon ground cinnamon /0.625G
- 1-pound skinless, boneless chicken breast halves cut into 2-inch pieces /450G
- 2 cloves garlic, minced
- 2 tablespoons lemon juice /30ML
- 2 tablespoons vegetable oil /30ML
- 3/4 teaspoon salt /3.75G

Instructions:

1) Add cardamom, cinnamon, allspice, pepper, oregano, salt, tomato paste, garlic, yogurt, vegetable oil, and fresh lemon juice in a Ziploc bag. Add chicken, mix, press to remove excess air, seal, and marinate inside refrigerator for 4 hours.
2) Thread chicken into skewers, place on skewer rack and cook in batches.
3) For 10 minutes, cook on 360° F or 183°C . Turn over skewer after 5 minutes.
4) Serve with a sprinkle of parsley and enjoy.

Nutrition Information:

- Calories per Serving: 297
- Carbs: 9.8g
- Protein: 34.3g
- Fat: 13.4g

Leftovers 'n Enchilada Bake

Servings per Recipe: 3

Cooking Time: 45 minutes

Ingredients:

- 1 egg
- 1/2 (15 ounces) can black beans, drained /450G
- 1/2 (15 ounces) can tomato sauce /450ML
- 1/2 (7.5 ounces) package corn bread mix /225G
- 1/2 cup shredded Mexican-style cheese blend, or even more to taste /65G
- 1/2 envelope taco seasoning mix
- 1/2-pound chicken tenderloins /225G
- 1-1/2 teaspoons vegetable oil /7.5G
- 2 tablespoons cream cheese /30G
- 2 tablespoons water /30ML
- 2-1/4 teaspoons chili powder /11.25G
- 3 tablespoons milk /45ML

Instructions:

1) Oil baking pan. Add chicken and cook for 5 minutes at 360° F or 183°C .

2) While stirring add the chili powder, taco seasoning mix, water, and tomato sauce. Cook for 10 minutes, continue mixing and turning the chicken. Keep stirring and turning chicken halfway through cooking time.
3) Remove chicken from pan and shred with two forks. Return to pan and stir in cream cheese and black beans. Mix well.
4) Top with Mexican cheese.
5) Whisk egg and milk until thoroughly beaten. Add cornbread mix and mix well. Pour over chicken.
6) Cover pan with foil.
7) Cook for additional 15 minutes. Remove foil and cook for 10 more minutes or until topping is lightly browned.
8) Let it sit for 5 minutes.
9) Serve and enjoy.

Nutrition Information:

- Calories per Serving: 487
- Carbs: 45.9g
- Protein: 31.2g
- Fat: 19.8g

Lemon-Aleppo Chicken

Servings per Recipe: 4

Cooking Time: 1 hour

Ingredients

- ¼ cup Aleppo-style pepper /32.5G
- ¼ cup fresh lemon juice /62.5ML
- ¼ cup oregano /32.5G
- 1 cup green olives, pitted and cracked /130G
- 1.4 cups chopped rosemary /182G
- 2 pounds whole chicken, backbones removed and butterflied /900G
- 6 cloves of garlic, minced
- Salt and pepper to taste

Instructions:

1) Place the chicken side up and slice the breasts. Press your hand against the breast bone to flatten the breast tissue or remove the bones altogether.
2) Season the boneless chicken with salt, pepper, garlic, pepper, rosemary, lemon juice, and oregano.
3) Allow to marinate inside the fridge for at least 12 hours.
4) Preheat the air fryer to 390° F or 199°C .
5) Place the grill pan accessory in the air fryer.

6) Place the chicken on the grill pan and place the olives across the chicken.
7) Grill for 1 hour and turn over the chicken every 10 minutes for even grilling.

Nutrition information:

- Calories per serving: 502
- Carbs:50.4 g
- Protein:37.6 g
- Fat: 16.6g

Lemon-Butter Battered Thighs

Serves: 8

Cooking Time: 35 minutes

Ingredients:

- ½ cup chicken stock /125ML
- 1 cup almond flour /130G
- 1 egg, beaten
- 1 onion, diced
- 2 pounds chicken thighs /900G
- 2 tablespoons capers /30G
- 3 tablespoons extra virgin olive oil /45ML
- 4 tablespoons butter /60G
- Juice from 2 lemons, freshly squeezed
- Salt and pepper to taste

Instructions:

1) Preheat the air fryer for 5 minutes.
2) Combine all ingredients in a baking dish. Mix well.
3) Place the baking dish in the air fryer chamber.
4) Cook for 35 minutes at 325° F or 163°C .

Nutrition information:

- Calories per serving: 386
- Carbohydrates: 3.7g

- Protein: 20.6g
- Fat: 32.1g

Lemon-Oregano Chicken BBQ

Servings per Recipe: 6

Cooking Time: 40 minutes

Ingredients:

- 1 tablespoon grated lemon zest /15G
- 2 tablespoons fresh lemon juice /30ML
- 2 tablespoons oregano, chopped /30G
- 3 pounds chicken breasts /1150G
- 4 cloves of garlic, minced
- Salt and pepper to taste

Instructions

1) Preheat the air fryer to 390° F or 199°C .
2) Place the grill pan in the air fryer.
3) Season the chicken with oregano, garlic, lemon zest, lemon juice, salt and pepper.
4) Grill for 40 minutes and flip every 10 minutes to grill evenly.

Nutrition information:

- Calories per serving: 388
- Carbs: 1.9g
- Protein: 47.5g
- Fat: 21.2g

Lemon-Parsley Chicken Packets

Servings per Recipe: 4

Cooking Time: 45 minutes

Ingredients:

- ¼ cup smoked paprika /32.5G
- ½ cup parsley leaves /65G
- ½ teaspoon liquid smoke seasoning /2.5ML
- 1 ½ tablespoon cayenne pepper /22.5G
- 2 pounds chicken thighs /900G
- 4 lemons, halved
- Salt and pepper to taste

Instructions:

1) Preheat the air fryer to 390° F or 199°C .
2) Place the grill pan inside the air fryer.
3) Place the chicken and season with paprika, liquid smoke seasoning, salt, pepper, and cayenne in a large foil.
4) Top with lemon and parsley.
5) Place in the grill and cook for 45 minutes.

Nutrition information:

- Calories per serving: 551
- Carbs: 10.4g
- Protein: 39.2g

- Fat: 39.1g

Malaysian Chicken Satay with Peanut Sauce

Servings per Recipe: 4

Cooking Time: 25 minutes

Ingredients:

- 1 tablespoon fish sauce /15ML
- 1 tablespoon lime juice /15ML
- 1 tablespoon white sugar /15G
- 1 tablespoon yellow curry powder /15G
- 1 teaspoon fish sauce /5G
- 1 teaspoon white sugar /5G
- 1/2 cup chicken broth /125ML
- 1/2 cup unsweetened coconut milk /125ML
- 1/2 teaspoon granulated garlic /2.5G
- 1/4 cup creamy peanut butter /32.5G
- 1-pound skinless, boneless chicken breasts, cut into strips /450G
- 2 tablespoons organic olive oil /30ML
- 2 teaspoons yellow curry powder /10G
- 3/4 cup unsweetened coconut milk /197ML

Instructions:

1) Mix garlic, 1 tsp fish sauce, 1 tsp sugar, 2 tsp. curry powder, and ½ cup coconut milk in a Ziploc bag. Add chicken and mix well to coat. Remove excess air and seal bag. Marinate for 120 minutes.
2) Skewer chicken and place on the skewer rack.
3) For 10 minutes, cook at 390° F or 199°C . Halfway through cooking time, turnover skewers.
4) Meanwhile, make peanut sauce by simmering the remaining coconut milk in a medium saucepan. Stir in curry powder and cook for 4 minutes. Add 1 tbsp fish sauce, lime juice, 1 tbsp sugar, peanut butter, and chicken broth. Mix well and cook until heated through. Transfer to a small bowl.
5) Serve with the peanut sauce and enjoy.

Nutrition Information:

- Calories per Serving: 482
- Carbs: 12.1g
- Protein: 31.7g
- Fat: 34.0g

Meat-Covered Boiled Eggs

Serves: 7

Cooking Time: 25 minutes

Ingredients:

¼ cup coconut flour /32.5G

1-pound ground beef /450G

2 eggs, beaten

2 tablespoons butter, melted /30ML

7 large eggs, boiled and peeled

Cooking spray

Salt and pepper to taste

Instructions:

1) Preheat mid-air fryer for 5 minutes.
2) Place the beaten eggs, ground beef, butter, and coconut flour in a mixing bowl. Season with salt and pepper to taste.
3) Coat the boiled eggs with all the meat mixture, place in the fridge to set for 120 minutes.
4) Grease the baking pan with cooking spray.
5) Place inside the air fryer basket.
6) Cook at 350° F or 177°C for 25 minutes.

Nutrition information:

- Calories per serving: 325
- Carbohydrates: 1.8g
- Protein: 21.4g
- Fat: 25.8g

Middle Eastern Chicken BBQ with Tzatziki Sauce

Servings per Recipe: 6

Cooking Time: 24 minutes

Ingredients:

- 1 1/2 pounds skinless, boneless chicken halves - cut into bite-sized pieces /675G
- 1 teaspoon dried oregano /5G
- 1/2 teaspoon salt /2.5G
- 1/4 cup essential olive oil /62.5ML
- 2 cloves garlic, minced
- 2 tablespoons lemon juice /30ML
- Tzatziki Dip Ingredients
- 1 (6 ounces) container plain Greek-style yogurt /180ML
- 1 tablespoon extra virgin olive oil /15ML
- 2 teaspoons white wine vinegar /10ML
- 1 clove garlic, minced
- 1 pinch of salt
- 1/2 cucumber - peeled, seeded, and grated

Instructions:

1) Mix all the Tzatziki dip Ingredients in a medium-sized bowl. Refrigerate for at least 120 minutes.

2) Mix salt, oregano, garlic, lemon juice, and organic olive oil in a bowl. Mix well. Add chicken, squeeze excess air, seal, and marinate for at least some hours.
3) Thread chicken into skewers and put on a skewer rack. Cook in batches.
4) For 12 minutes, cook on 360° F or 183°C . Halfway through cooking time, turnover skewers and baste with marinade.
5) Serve and enjoy with Tzatziki dip.

Nutrition Information:

- Calories per Serving: 264
- Carbs: 2.6g
- Protein: 25.5g
- Fat: 16.8g

Mixed Vegetable Breakfast Frittata

Servings per Recipe: 6

Cooking Time: 45 minutes

Ingredients:

- ½-pound breakfast sausage /225G
- 1 cup cheddar cheese shredded /130G
- 1 teaspoon kosher salt /5G
- 1/2 cup milk or cream /125ML
- 1/2 teaspoon black pepper /2.5G
- 6 eggs
- 8-ounces frozen mixed vegetables (sweet peppers, broccoli, etc.), thawed /240G

Instructions:

1) Oil baking pan lightly with cooking spray. Cook the breakfast sausage at 360° F or 183°C for 10 minutes crush the sausage until you get ground meat. After 5 minutes crush again. Remove excess fat when cooing is done.
2) Stir in thawed mixed vegetables and cook for 7 minutes or until heated through, stirring halfway through cooking time.
3) Whisk eggs, cream, salt, and pepper well in a bowl.
4) Evenly spread the vegetable mixture in the air fryer basket and pour in the egg mixture. Cover pan with foil.

5) Cook for 15 minutes, remove foil and continue cooking for additional 5-10 minutes or until eggs are well cooked.
6) Serve and enjoy.

Nutrition Information:

- Calories per Serving: 187
- Carbs: 7.0g
- Protein: 15.0g
- Fat: 11.0g

Mushroom 'n Coconut Cream Quiche

Serves: 8

Cooking Time: 20 minutes

Ingredients:

- ¼ cup coconut cream /62.5ML
- ½ cup almond flour /65G
- ½ cup mushroom, sliced /65G
- ½ onion, chopped
- 1 tablespoon chives, chopped /15G
- 2 tablespoons coconut oil /30ML
- 4 eggs, beaten
- Salt and pepper to taste

Instructions:

1) Preheat the air fryer for 5 minutes.
2) Add the almond flour and coconut oil.
3) Put the almond flour mixture at the bottom of the baking dish.
4) Place inside air fryer and cook for 5 minutes.
5) Meanwhile, add other ingredients to the mixing bowl. Mix well.
6) Take the crust out and pour over the egg mixture.
7) Put the baking dish back into the air fryer and cook for 15 minutes at 350° F or 177°C .

Nutrition information:

- Calories per serving: 125
- Carbohydrates: 2.2g
- Protein: 4.8g
- Fat: 10.8g

Naked Cheese, Chicken Stuffing 'n Green Beans

Servings per Recipe: 3

Cooking Time: 20 minutes

Ingredients:

- 1 cup cooked, cubed chicken breast meat /130G
- 1/2 (10.75 ounces) can condense cream of chicken soup /322.5ML
- 1/2 (14.5 ounces) can green beans, drained /435G
- 1/2 cup shredded Cheddar cheese /65G
- 6-ounce unseasoned dry bread stuffing mix /180G
- salt and pepper to taste

Instructions:

1) Mix pepper, salt, soup, and chicken in a medium bowl.
2) Make the stuffing according to package directions for cooking.
3) Oil the baking pan of the air fryer with cooking spray. Evenly spread chicken mixture at the bottom of the pan. Top evenly with stuffing. Sprinkle cheese on the top.
4) Cover the pan with foil.
5) For 15 minutes, cook at 390° F or 199°C .
6) Remove foil and cook for 5 minutes at 390° F until tops are lightly browned.

7) Serve and enjoy.

Nutrition Information:

- Calories per Serving: 418
- Carbs: 48.8g
- Protein: 27.1g
- Fat: 12.7g

Non-Fattening Breakfast Frittata

Servings per Recipe: 2

Cooking Time: 15 minutes

Ingredients:

- ¼ cup sliced mushrooms /32.5G
- ¼ cup sliced tomato /32.5G
- 1 cup egg whites
- 2 Tbsp chopped fresh chives /30G
- 2 Tbsp skim milk /30ML
- Salt and Black pepper, to taste

Instructions:

1) Grease the baking pan of the air fryer with cooking spray.
2) Spread mushrooms and tomato at the bottom of the pan.
3) Whisk egg whites, milk, chives, pepper and salt. Pour into baking pan.
4) For 15 minutes, cook at 330° F or 166°C.
5) Remove the basket and allow it to sit for a minute.
6) Serve and enjoy.

Nutrition Information:

- Calories per Serving: 231
- Carbs: 35.1g
- Protein: 21.5g

- Fat: 0.5g

Orange-Tequila Glazed Chicken

Servings per Recipe: 6

Cooking Time: 40 minutes

Ingredients:

- ¼ cup tequila /62.5ML
- 1 shallot, minced
- 1/3 cup orange juice /83ML
- 2 tablespoons brown sugar /30G
- 2 tablespoons honey /30ML
- 2 tablespoons whole coriander seeds /30G
- 3 cloves of garlic, minced
- 3 pounds chicken breasts /1150G
- Salt and pepper to taste

Instructions:

1) Place all ingredients in a Ziploc bag, shake to mix. Place in the fridge for some hours.
2) Preheat mid-air fryer to 390° F or 199°C .
3) Place the grill pan in the air fryer.
4) Grill the chicken for at least 40 minutes
5) Flip the chicken over every 10 Minutes.
6) Meanwhile, pour the marinade in the saucepan and simmer to thicken.
7) Brush the chicken with the sauce before serving.

Nutrition information:

- Calories per serving: 440
- Carbs: 11.2g
- Protein: 48.1g
- Fat: 22.5g

Oregano-Thyme Rubbed Thighs

Servings per Recipe: 4

Cooking Time: 11 minutes

Ingredients

- 4 bone-in chicken thighs with skin
- 1/8 teaspoon garlic salt /0.625G
- 1/8 teaspoon onion salt /0.625G
- 1/8 teaspoon dried oregano /0.625G
- 1/8 teaspoon ground thyme /0.625G
- 1/8 teaspoon paprika /0.625G
- 1/8 teaspoon ground black pepper /0.625G

Instructions:

1) Lightly grease baking pan of air fryer with oil of your choosing. Use a cooking spray to grease. Place chicken with skin side touching the bottom of the pan.
2) Mix pepper, paprika, thyme, oregano, onion salt, and garlic salt properly. Sprinkle this mixture on the chicken.
3) Cook at 390° F or 199°C .for 1 minute.
4) Turnover chicken while rubbing on the bottom and sides of the pan for more seasoning.
5) Cook for 10 minutes at 390° F or 199°C .
6) Serve and enjoy.

Nutrition Information:

- Calories per Serving: 185
- Carbs: 0.2g
- Protein: 19.2g
- Fat: 11.9g

Over the Top Chicken Enchiladas

Servings per Recipe: 3

Cooking Time: 50 minutes

Ingredients:

- 1/2 (1.25 ounce) package mild taco seasoning mix /37.5G
- 1/2 (10 ounces) can enchilada sauce /300ML
- 1/2 (10.75 ounces) can condensed cream of chicken soup /322.5ML
- 1/2 (4 ounces) can chopped green chilies, drained /120G
- 1/2 (6 ounces) can sliced black olives /180G
- 1/2 bunch green onions, chopped, divided
- 1/2 cup sour cream /125ML
- 1/2 cup water /125ML
- 1/2 small onion, chopped
- 1/2 teaspoon lime juice /2.5ML
- 1/4 teaspoon garlic powder /1.25G
- 1/4 teaspoon onion powder 1.25G
- 1/8 teaspoon chili powder /0.625G
- 1-1/2 cups Cheddar cheese, shredded, divided /195G
- 1-1/2 teaspoons butter /7.5G
- 1-pound skinless, boneless chicken white meat, cooked and shredded /450G
- 3 (12 inches) flour tortillas

Instructions:

1) Grease the baking pan of the air fryer with butter. Add onion and then for 5 minutes, cook on 360° F or 183°C .
2) Stir in water, green onions, taco seasoning, green chilies, and shredded chicken. Cook for another 10 minutes.
3) Stir in garlic powder, onion powder, and lime juice. Cook for 5 minutes or more.
4) Add chili powder, sour cream, and cream of chicken soup. Pour a cup of the mixture into the baking pan and mix well.
5) Evenly divide the chicken mixture in the flour tortillas, sprinkle with half in the cheese and roll.
6) Pour the remaining soup mixture into an air fryer baking pan. Place tortillas seam side down. Pour enchilada sauce on the top and sprinkle remaining cheese.
7) Cover pan with foil.
8) Cook for another 20 minutes, remove foil and continue cooking another 10 minutes.
9) Serve and enjoy.

Nutrition Information:

- Calories per Serving: 706
- Carbs: 52.5g
- Protein: 42.2g
- Fat: 36.3g

Paprika-Cumin Rubbed Chicken Tenderloin

Serves: 6

Cooking Time: 25 minutes

Ingredients:

- ¼ cup coconut flour /32.5G
- ¼ cup extra virgin olive oil /62.5ML
- ½ teaspoon garlic powder /2.5G
- ½ teaspoon ground cumin /2.5G
- ½ teaspoon onion powder /2.5G
- ½ teaspoon smoked paprika /2.5G
- 1-pound chicken tenderloins /450G
- Salt and pepper to taste

Instructions:

1) Preheat mid-air fryer for 5 minutes.
2) Soak the chicken tenderloins in essential olive oil.
3) Mix the remainder of the ingredients and stir with your hands to combine everything.
4) Place the chicken pieces inside the air fryer basket.
5) Cook for 25 minutes at 325° F or 163°C .

Nutrition information:

- Calories per serving: 430

- Carbohydrates: 4.1g
- Protein:27.3g
- Fat: 33.8g

Pasta with Turkey-Basil Red Sauce

Servings per Recipe: 3

Cooking Time: 35 minutes

Ingredients:

- 1 teaspoon white sugar /5G
- 1/2 cup tomato sauce /125ML
- 1/2-pound lean ground turkey /225G
- 1/4 teaspoon dried basil /1.25G
- 2 cloves garlic, minced
- 7-ounce can stewed, diced tomatoes /210G
- 8-ounce bow tie pasta, cooked following manufacturer's Instructions /240G

Instructions:

1) Using a cooking spray, lightly grease the baking pan of the air fryer. Add ground turkey and garlic.
2) For 10 Minutes, cook at 360° F or 183°C . After 5 minutes stir and crumble ground turkey.
3) Stir in basil, sugar, tomato sauce, and stewed tomatoes. Mix well.
4) Cook for another 10 minutes, mixing well halfway through cooking time.
5) Stir in cooked pasta and mix well.
6) Cook for another 5 minutes, mix well.

7) Serve and enjoy.

Nutrition Information:

- Calories per Serving: 316
- Carbs: 46.9g
- Protein: 18.3g
- Fat: 6.1g

Pepper-Salt Egg ‘n Spinach Casserole

Serves: 6

Cooking Time: 20 Minutes

Ingredients:

- ½ cup red onion, chopped /65G
- 1 cup mushrooms, sliced /130G
- 1 red bell pepper, seeded and julienned
- 3 cups frozen spinach, chopped /390G
- 3 egg whites, beaten
- 4 eggs, beaten
- Salt and pepper to taste

Instructions:

1) Preheat the air fryer for 5 minutes.
2) Combine the eggs and egg whites in a bowl. Whisk until fluffy.
3) Place the rest of the ingredients inside a baking dish and pour the egg mixture.
4) Place inside the air fryer chamber.
5) Cook for 20 minutes at 310° F or 155°C .

Nutrition information:

- Calories per serving: 170
- Carbohydrates: 4.8g

- Protein: 9.3g
- Fat: 12.6g

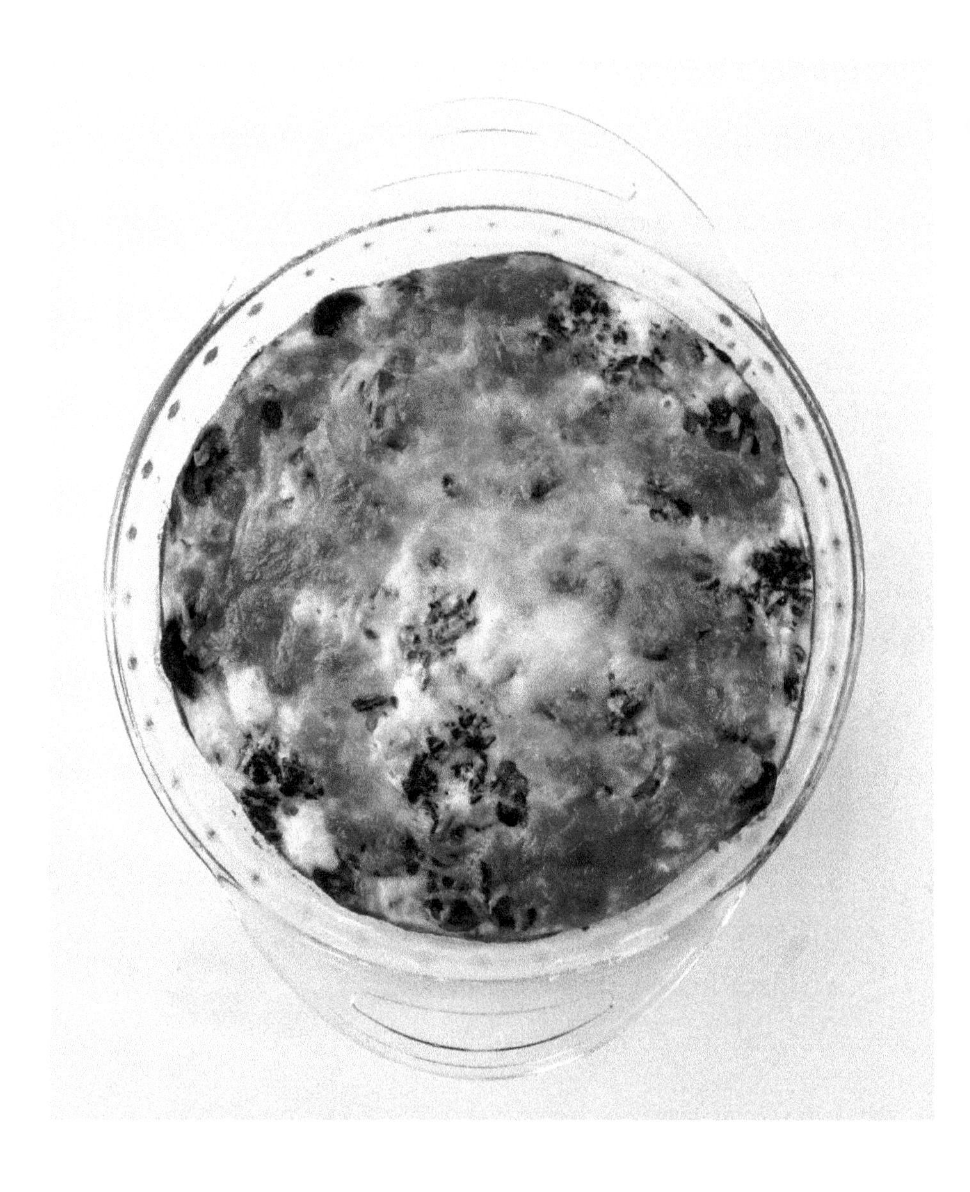

Peppery Lemon-Chicken Breast

Serves: 1

Cooking Time:

Ingredients:

- 1 chicken breast
- 1 teaspoon minced garlic /5G
- 2 lemons, rinds and juice reserved
- Salt and pepper to taste

Instructions:

1) Preheat mid-air fryer.
2) Place all ingredients in a baking dish that will fit within the air fryer.
3) Place inside the air fryer basket.
4) Close and cook for 20 minutes at 400° F or 205°C .

Nutrition information:

- Calories per serving: 539
- Carbohydrates: 11.8g
- Protein: 61.8g
- Fat: 27.2g

Pineapple Juice-Soy Sauce Marinated Chicken

Servings per Recipe: 5

Cooking Time: 20 Minutes

Ingredients:

- 3 tablespoons light soy sauce /45ML
- 1-pound chicken white meat tenderloins or strips /450G
- 1/2 cup pineapple juice /125ML
- 1/4 cup packed brown sugar /32.5G

Instructions:

1) Boil pineapple juice, brown sugar, and soy sauce. Transfer to a large bowl. Stir in chicken and pineapple. Let it marinate in the fridge for an hour or more.
2) Thread pineapple and chicken alternatively in skewers. Place on skewer rack.
3) For 10 minutes, cook on 360° F or 183°C . Halfway through cooking time, turnover chicken and baste with marinade.
4) Serve and enjoy.

Nutrition Information:

- Calories per Serving: 157
- Carbs: 14.7g

- Protein: 19.4g
- Fat: 2.2g

Quick 'n Easy Brekky Eggs 'n Cream

Serves: 2

Cooking Time: 15 minutes

Ingredients:

- 2 eggs
- 2 tablespoons coconut cream /30ML
- A dash of Spanish paprika
- Salt and pepper to taste

Instructions:

1) Preheat mid-air fryer for 5 minutes.
2) Place the eggs and coconut cream in a bowl. Season with salt and pepper to taste then whisk until fluffy.
3) Pour into greased pan and sprinkle with Spanish paprika.
4) Place in the air fryer.
5) Bake for 15 minutes at 350° F or 177°C .

Nutrition information:

- Calories per serving:178.1
- Carbohydrates: 1.1g
- Protein: 9.9g
- Fat: 14.9g

Quick 'n Easy Garlic Herb Wings

Servings per Recipe: 4

Cooking Time: 35 minutes

Ingredients

- ¼ cup chopped rosemary /32.5G
- 2 pounds chicken wings /900G
- 6 medium garlic cloves, grated
- Salt and pepper to taste

Instructions:

1) Season the chicken with garlic, rosemary, salt and pepper.
2) Preheat mid-air fryer to 390° F or 199°C .
3) Place the chicken in the grill pan, place the pan in the air fryer.
4) Grill for 35 minutes and turn over the chicken every 10 minutes.

Nutrition information:

- Calories per serving: 287
- Carbs: 2.9g
- Protein: 50.4g
- Fat: 8.2g

Radish Hash Browns with Onion-Paprika Spice

Serves: 6

Cooking Time: 10

Ingredients

- ¼ teaspoon ground black pepper /1.25G
- ½ teaspoon paprika /2.5G
- ¾ teaspoon salt /3.75G
- 1 onion, chopped
- 1 teaspoon garlic powder /5G
- 1 teaspoon onion powder /5G
- 1-pound radish, peeled and grated /450G
- 3 tablespoon coconut oil /45ML

Instructions:

1) Preheat the air fryer for 5 minutes.
2) Place all ingredients in the mixing bowl. Mix well.
3) Form patties using your hands and set each patty in the air fryer basket.
4) Grease with cooking spray before closing the air fryer.
5) Cook for 10 Minutes at 350° F or 177°C until crispy.

Nutrition information:

- Calories per serving: 81

- Carbohydrates: 5.7g
- Protein: 0.9g
- Fat: 6.1g

Reuben Style Chicken Roll-up

Servings per Recipe: 2

Cooking Time: 15 minutes

Ingredients

- 1/4 teaspoon garlic salt /1.25G
- 1/4 teaspoon pepper /1.25G
- 2 boneless skinless chicken breast halves (4 ounces or 120G each)
- 2 slices deli corned beef
- 2 slices swirled rye and pumpernickel bread
- 2 slices Swiss cheese
- 2 tablespoons Thousand Island salad dressing /30G
- Additional Thousand Island salad dressing, optional

Instructions:

1) Tear bread into 2-inch pieces, put in a blender and blend until crushed. Transfer into a shallow bowl.
2) With meal mallet, pound chicken to ¼ inch thick. Season with pepper and salt. Top chicken with corned beef and cheese. Roll chicken and secure ends with a toothpick.
3) Brush chicken with dressing and dip in crumbs until completely covered.
4) Lightly grease baking pan of air fryer with cooking spray. Place rollups.

5) Cook for 15 minutes at 330° F or 166°C preheated air fryer.
6) Turnover rollups and continue cooking for an additional 10 minutes.
7) Serve with extra dressing and enjoy.

Nutrition Information:

- Calories per Serving: 317
- Carbs: 18.0g
- Protein: 32.0g
- Fat: 13.0g

Roast Chicken Recipe from Africa

Servings per Recipe: 6

Cooking Time: 45 minutes

Ingredients:

- ¼ cup fresh freshly squeezed lemon juice /62.5ML
- ½ cup Piri Piri sauce /125ML
- 1 large shallots, quartered
- 1-inch fresh ginger, peeled and sliced thinly
- 3 cloves of garlic, minced
- 3 pounds chicken breasts
- Salt and pepper to taste

Instructions:

1) Preheat the air fryer to 390° F or 199°C .
2) Place the grill pan in the air fryer.
3) On a large foil, add the chicken top along with the rest with the Ingredients.
4) Fold the foil and secure the edges.
5) Grill for 45 minutes.

Nutrition information:

- Calories per serving: 395
- Carbs: 3.4g
- Protein: 47.9g
- Fat: 21.1g

Salsa on Chicken-Rice Bake

Servings per Recipe: 4

Cooking Time: 65 minutes

Ingredients:

- 2 skinless, boneless chicken white meat halves
- 1 cup shredded Monterey Jack cheese /130G
- 1 cup shredded Cheddar cheese /130G
- 1/2 (10.75 ounces) can condensed cream of chicken soup /322.5ML
- 1/2 (10.75 ounces) can condensed cream of mushroom soup 322.5ML
- 1/2 onion, chopped
- 1-1/3 cups water /333ML
- 2/3 cup uncooked white rice /87G
- 3/4 cup mild salsa /98G

Instructions:

1) Use a cooking spray to grease lightly the baking pan. Add water, rice, and chicken. Cover with foil and cook for 25 minutes at 360° F or 183°C .
2) Remove foil and take away chicken and cut into bite-sized pieces. Fluff rice and transfer to a plate.

3) Place the cheese in a bowl and mix well. Place the salsa onion, cream of mushroom, and cream of chicken in a bowl and mix well.
4) In same air fryer baking pan evenly spread ½ of rice on the bottom, top with ½ of chicken, ½ of soup mixture, after which ½ of cheese. Repeat layering process.
5) Cover with foil and cook for another 25 minutes. Remove foil and cook until the top is browned.
6) Serve and enjoy.

Nutrition Information:

- Calories per Serving: 475
- Carbs: 34.8g
- Protein: 30.0g
- Fat: 23.9g

Salsa Verde over Grilled Chicken

Servings per Recipe: 2

Cooking Time: 40 minutes

Ingredients:

- ½ red onion, chopped
- ½ teaspoon chili powder /2.5G
- 1 jalapeno thinly sliced
- 1 jar salsa verde, divided
- 1-pound boneless skinless chicken breasts /450G
- 2 cloves of garlic, minced
- 2 tablespoons chopped cilantro /30ML
- 2 tablespoons extra virgin organic olive oil /30ML
- 4 slices Monterey Jack cheese
- Juice from ½ lime
- Lime wedges for serving

Instructions

1) Add half the salsa verde, extra virgin olive oil, lime juice, garlic, chili powder and chicken in a Ziploc bag. Allow to marinate in the fridge for 120 minutes.
2) Preheat the air fryer to 390° F or 199°C .
3) Place the grill pan in the air fryer.
4) Grill the chicken for 40 minutes.
5) Flip the chicken over every 10 minutes to grill evenly.

6) Serve the chicken using cheese, jalapeno, red onion, cilantro, and lime wedges.

Nutrition information:

- Calories per serving: 541
- Carbs: 4.5g
- Protein: 65.3g
- Fat: 29.1g

Salted Meaty Egg Frittata

Serves: 3

Cooking Time: 20 Minutes

Ingredients:

- ½ pound ground beef /450G
- 1 onion, chopped
- 3 cloves of garlic, minced
- 3 eggs, beaten
- 3 tablespoons extra virgin olive oil /45ML
- Salt and pepper to taste

Instructions:

1) Place pan on medium heat, add oil.
2) Sauté the garlic and onion until fragrance is released.
3) Add the ground beef and sauté for 5 minutes or until lightly golden. Set aside.
4) Preheat the air fryer for 5 minutes.
5) Combine the rest of the ingredients in a mixing bowl.
6) Place the sautéed beef in the baking dish that may fit into the air fryer chamber.
7) Pour on the egg mixture.
8) Cook for 20 minutes at 320° F or 160°C .

Nutrition information:

- Calories per serving: 461
- Carbohydrates: 6.8g
- Protein: 28.9g
- Fat: 35.4g

Savory Chives 'n Bacon Frittata

Serves: 4

Cooking Time: 15

Ingredients:

- 1 tablespoon chives /15G
- 6 eggs, beaten
- 6 uncured bacon, fried and crumbled
- Salt and pepper to taste

Instructions:

1) Preheat mid-air fryer for 5 minutes.
2) Mix all ingredients in a mixing bowl.
3) Pour the condiment into a greased baking dish.
4) Close and cook for 15 minutes at 350° F or 177°C .

Nutrition information:

- Calories per serving: 255
- Carbohydrates: 3.6g
- Protein: 15.6g
- Fat: 19.8g

Shishito Pepper Rubbed Wings

Servings per Recipe: 6

Cooking Time: 30 Minutes

Ingredients:

- 1 ½ cups shishito peppers, pureed /195G
- 2 tablespoons sesame oil /30ML
- 3 pounds chicken wings /1150G
- Salt and pepper to taste

Instructions:

1) Place all ingredients inside a Ziploc bowl and allow to marinate for at least 2 hours inside the fridge.
2) Preheat mid-air fryer to 390° F or 199°C .
3) Place the grill pan in the air fryer.
4) Grill for at least 30 minutes flipping the chicken every 5 minutes and basting using the remaining sauce.

Nutrition information:

- Calories per serving: 321
- Carbs: 1.7g
- Protein: 50.2g
- Fat: 12.6g

Soy-Honey Glazed Chicken Kebabs

Servings per Recipe: 8

Cooking Time: 36 minutes

Ingredients:

- 1 clove garlic
- 1 red sweet peppers, cut into 2-inch pieces
- 1/8 teaspoon ground black pepper /0.625G
- 2 tablespoons and two teaspoons honey /40ML
- 2 tablespoons and two teaspoons soy sauce /40ML
- 2 tablespoons vegetable oil /30ML
- 2-1/2 small onions, cut into 2-inch pieces
- 4 skinless, boneless chicken halves cut into 1-inch cubes

Instructions

1) Mix pepper, soy sauce, honey, and oil. Transfer ¼ of the marinade to a bowl for basting. Add chicken to the bowl and coat. Add pepper, onion, and garlic. Mix well to blend. Let it marinate for a couple of hours.
2) Thread vegetables and chicken alternatively into skewers and place them on the skewer rack in the air fryer.
3) For 12 minutes, cook at 360° F or 183°C . After 6 minutes of cooking, baste with marinade sauce and turnover skewers.
4) Serve and enjoy.

Nutrition Information:

- Calories per Serving: 179
- Carbs: 12.4g
- Protein: 17.4g
- Fat: 6.6g

Spinach 'n Bacon Egg Cups

Serves: 4

Cooking Time: 10

Ingredients

- ¼ cup spinach, chopped finely /32.5G
- 1 bacon strip, fried and crumbled
- 3 tablespoons butter /45G
- 4 eggs, beaten
- Salt and pepper to taste

Instructions:

1) Preheat the air fryer for 5 minutes.
2) Combine the eggs, butter, and spinach in a mixing bowl. Season with salt and pepper to taste.
3) Grease a cooking pan with a cooking spray and pour the egg mixture inside.
4) Sprinkle with bacon bits.
5) Place the pan in the air fryer.
6) Cook for 10 minutes at 350° F or 177°C .

Nutrition information:

- Calories per serving: 214
- Carbohydrates: 2.2g
- Protein: 9.4g

- Fat: 18.6g

Lightning Source UK Ltd.
Milton Keynes UK
UKHW020743150621
385540UK00005B/43